# MY MUSINGS

## A COLLECTION OF MY THOUGHTS

### BY

Dr. Prema Rajagopalan, MD, DA

Consultant Anesthesiologist, Dindigul, Tamil Nadu

Copyright © 2024 Prema Rajagopalan

All Rights Reserved.

# Author's Note

 not a gifted poet. I just started writing during pandemic isolation. My friends and well-
ers encouraged me to write more. My language proficiency in English and Tamil is very
le. They may not be considered "poems" by veteran poets. I wanted to write about the evils
e society, day to day miseries faced by the poor strata, and many more topics that touched
heart.

dicate these poems to my parents and sisters who would be proud of me from above.

nk my daughters, brother and husband who worked hard to bring out this book.


 book is a compilation of some of the English poems I wrote. Most of these were written
ng Covid, so the reader is requested to read them in the context of the emotions of that
od.

ny of the poems are in the Indian context, they may not apply in other countries.


*Prema Rajagopalan*

# TABLE OF CONTENTS

# Foreword

Dr Prema Rajagopalan is a practicing anesthetist in Dindigul Tamil Nadu

I have known Prema for over 40 years. She started as a young medico in JIPMER , ing her dream to become an anesthetist. After her postgraduation she joined the Tamil Nadu ernment service as consultant anesthetist. As an anesthetist, her job was in the grim environs n operation theatre, where the sounds of silence were supreme. But even behind the mask she ted a smile always as if to disperse the eery air and the anxiety of her patients and eagues.

As a young confident energetic anesthetist, she shuffled home and hospital, patients and 'ession with poise and composure

She was married to Dr Chandrasekar, a capable, skilled surgeon who supplemented her arkable career with his own. They had two girls who grew up in the environs of home and pital but decided to pursue their own paths and moved to the US.

Upon superannuation Dr Prema continued her services in various hospitals until covid med the breaks on her career.

Then came an awakening, the rise of a dormant passion in her. She quickly transformed n her profession to her passion that was poetry. She began to pen down her pent up thoughts diverse matters ranging from trivia to serious, social issues to mundane topics dotted with her dical and professional experiences. Some of her poetry reflected her innate values which had undertone of societal inequalities and injustices. These were possibly influenced by her sister social activist .

Her passion for poetry grew with the pandemic and has continued ever since and is on an rend. She recently hit a century- 100 bilingual poems, indicating her proficiency in English l Tamil. I end with my own four liner!

A pretty lass, doctor from Dindigul

An anesthetist, who never was dull

Worked with a smile, put all at ease

Took to poetry like chalk and cheese?

From daughters' day to doctors day

To speak her mind, wide was her array

She just reached a 100, kudos to her

*-Dr. Renuka Srinivasan, JIPMER, Pondicherry*

# Healthcare related poems

# Doctors' day

This day is too significant a day, sure,

Than ever before, celebrated every year,

In memory of Dr. B.C Roy,

India's famous physician from Bengal,


All those years are gone,

When doctors were honored,

Today they are only cornered.


When patients were loyal and thankful,

With peace and were grateful.


The trust was mutual,

True and factual.


Doctors never feared patients,

Dutiful with devotion.


Today, they are treated like dogs,

Bashed, beaten up by logs.


Their dignity, humanity should be preserved,

Their safety also to be ensured.


They slogged round the clock,

To bring patients' lives back.

With recognition from none,

With only humiliation, full duties done,


We don't need celebration!

We don't wait for appreciation.


We don't expect rewards,

We never can become Gods,

We are only humans, Lord,

What's the point, getting mad,

We too feel sad(for deaths)


Show us some understanding,

Stop all the misunderstanding.


Virus seems too hard,

Vaccines will save all, dear God.


Patience needed, patients our friends,

Pity us please, we plead you to end,

The assaults on doctors.


Happy doctors' day celebrated,

Only when doctors are honoured.


Will wait until then,

With my fellowmen

# Euthanasia (Mercy killing)

Ever debated issue, for many years
Never concluded, our end-stage fears,
Switzerland, Netherlands, Mapleland
New Zealand, To name a few lands
Relieved their citizens, terminally ill
Legalised their will, not a kill

Many a terms, for end of life state
 voluntary, involuntary…passive, active,too many to debate
Parents let us choose our school
Freedom enjoyed, very, very cool
Freedom to choose our career,
Freedom to choose our life partner
Freedom to decide the way we live,
Nay, No freedom to choose the way we die

When terminal illness engulfs me
When I am unable to poo and pee
Will should save me, and let me go
Tubes, lines all over me,
Throw them all, let me go free

Obstetricians, mothers decide D.O.B
Let me decide my D.O.D.
With mercy killing, option willed by me

Kith and kin, please hear my plea

Free me from pain, suffering,

For, all creations have an expiry date

Vegetative state, never for me,

Dejected life, not my cup of tea

# Front line heroes

They strive hard to become doctors
Crossing many hurdles, after many many exams,
Cream of the country, sure they are,
Dreams so many, dreamt about future

Six years of long journey,
At the end to see some decent money
They have a family too, to care
Aspire to settle down,adding few more years
PG degree seems to be their only dream
Many more years, they add, to join the mainstream
Young residents, sacrificed all,
Left their loved ones, to save us all,
Salaries paid, only pittance,
Struggle hard to achieve success

Corona virus killed so many
But they continue with their brave journey

None to offer them rental houses
None welcome them, no warmth,
Our brotherhood, their eyes with tears
Many sad stories, we hear with fear
Ophthal pg never sees eyes,
Surgery pg's, nil knowledge of tumour size

Never have they held any knives

Radiology pg, learns only lung scans

Anesthesia pg's, intubate ICU patients,

He is yet to see the operation theaters

With all the electives postponed,

He learns nothing, except to manage oxygen shortage


Two precious years of PG times,

Lost in their lives, due to corona duties

They are the victims of relatives' (patients) outbursts

Physical assaults, they shed tears

Long hours in those PPEs

Postponing their nature calls

No food, no drinks, nothing at all


Senior consultants, sitting at home

Juniors' duties doubled and doomed

Duty doctors 24x7 work

Their personal lives really suck


Nurses, workers, all of them,

Worse than doctors, a real shame

Applaud our front-line heroes

With all our might

Support them, when they fight for their genuine rights

They are our saviours, join all hands

Give all benefits, they are worth, after all

They are our heroes, they stand tall

11

# Mixopaths

Ayush doctors to practice allopathy,
Allow them not, no sympathy.


We have respect for Indian medicine,
We request them to stick onto theirs, not a sin.


Chronic minor ailments so many,
Clear borders drawn, let them not get loony.


Prove your might in your chosen field,
Poor patients get cheated, consider their needs.


Allopaths are scarce in villages they say,
Ayush doctors also scarce, they dispense from far away.


A country where non specialists (M.B.B.S) are never allowed into surgery,
After five and a half years of complete study,


They are licensed to treat only generally,
They cannot enter any specialty territory,


Exit exams to pass, for qualified allopaths,
Enter those unqualified into practice, the mixopaths.


Exposure of allopaths with patients,
Ever so many with relevant investigations,
Many strange ills, still untreatable,

Many research, evidence based, incomparable.

One and a half years, our dissections on human body,
One after another, the parts we studied.

Residency, postgraduation in the specialties,
Critical care, anesthesia and casualties.

We spend nine years on overall training,
We forget family, youth for qualifying.

Are we marching towards pre independence days?
AUs, L.M.Ps, treated patients, no ways.

Patients sue, beat up the allopaths,
Can they do the same with mixopaths?
Will they be accountable for mixing "paths"?

Their hands-on experience too limited,
With small number of patients, they see, not committed,

The long queues in government hospitals,
They wait to meet allopath specialists,
Though we have siddha wing,
They hesitate to visit them, even for minor ailments.

Will you consult a mixopath,
When you have cataract?

Will you meet an oncologist,

With your cancer spreading, or mixologist?


Let the nation have separate Ayush hospitals,

Let patients decide on their specialists.


Please don't mix them with allopaths,

Poor doctors! They travel a separate path,

Medical ethics allow no crossing of paths.


Complications, if any, allopaths manage,

Confused mixopaths, with nil knowledge.

# Organ donation

Noble deed of organ donation,

Enable youth to live on with no frustration,

Longer years they live before their destination,

Lovely last gift by a donor, expect no reciprocation.


Single donor can do eight organ donations,

So many factors excluded, sacrifice of the brain-dead patients.


(Symbol of organ donation)Green ribbon groups do a lot of motivation,

Give them your hand in appreciation.


First one in 1954, of kidney of cadaver,

Followed by heart 1967, first ever,

(Our) First kidney transplant 1967 in Mumbai

First heart trasplant 1994, In Aiims Delhi


Transplant can be from cadaver,

True relatives can become live donors,

Tissue transplant done across the world,

Tears secreting eyes, lungs, pancreas, skin too shared.

Swap donation between two families,

Some recent concept, welcome hopefully.


Autograft, Allograft, Isograft many more grafts,

Arrive by air ambulance or others before six hours pass.


When doctors declare brain death,

Wee hours not to waste after cardiac death.

Donor is sure viewed as hero,

Donation of his organs, he lives on to see tomorrow.


Sees the world through unknown recipient,

Sharing his body, sure he is very different.

Many sick ones waiting for donors,

Move on with organs, do them honors.


The last precious gift to fellow men,

The donor lives on after death, Amen!


The remnants of body, after organ donation,

They can be buried, burnt with no discrimination.


Those unlucky ones on long wait lists,

They die soon, before their turn, before they become fit.


Tissue donations, with banks upcoming,

To recycle ourselves, quite heart warming.


We have done many donations,

With food, clothes, money and many collections,

Will the last one be organ donation?

All religions support this notion,

All myths dropped, when we reach a point of no return.

# ICU blues

A place to learn life's philosophies,
As an intensivist, as a patient, and as a relative.


ICUs of our government hospitals,
Non-stop surge of critical patients.


Half dead, heart dead, they enter in a swarm,
Hanging, poisons, snake bites, accidents never to calm.


Shortage of beds we always faced,
Stomach wash, scorpion stings, sorrowful scenes, in quick pace,


Ventilator shortages to be managed,
With "To and fro canisters" (hand ventilation) patients salvaged.


Some scenes of corporate ICUs,
Shortage none, to ensue.
Problem of plenty in these ones
Paid through their nose, with hospital bill woes.


NRI sons and daughters though,
Anxiety over the hefty bills they show.


The agonies that sick ones undergo,
Tubes, catheters with oxygen flow,
Tracheostomy suctions, patients' description,

Trachea on fire with every insertion.


ICUs with all the cacophony,

Miseries, cries, make one loony.


Doctors never to give upon patients,

Do their best to save, their devotion,

Demigods, they are not, only work with dedication.


Elders of my family, left from ICUs,

End of life after peaceful journey,

Entered heaven in their trance.


I can't end without mention of my sister,

She vanished in thin air, with none to care,

She bypassed hospital, ICU, was she clever?

Straight to heaven, where she lives for ever,


ICU services, save many souls,

I am not game for ICU, not my goal,

I have my will, when I go still,


I may not be tied to machines,

I would go with no ICU scenes.

# Cesarean sections

Month of April signifies C sections,

US saw in 1794 the first one,

Centuries back Luxemberg saw many successful ones,

In the 13 th century with mortality none,


Drs Jesse and Humphry teamed up for section on Jesse's wife,

Elizabeth the patient experienced the cut with knife,


Jesse performed section at his barn,

With instruments, barrels in his lawn,


His wife and baby Bennet survived though,

He dared not publish his crude way, oh no!


Planned and emergency sections,

Save babies with safety precautions,


That curved incision from right to left,

Neatly hides into the bikini, do their best,


Patient prepared with that green gown,

All set to receive her little one,


Pushed to O.T table with those flood lights,

Sounds of instruments monitors, she sure waits,


Her eyepads not tightly tied,

She sees things through sides,


Anesthesia is mostly a poke at her back,

Unaware of things, she is shocked,


She is wide awake when the surgeon cuts,

Anesthetist asks her to take deep breaths,


Within minutes that miracle happens,

Baby out, she is into cloud nine,


Nurse cleans up the newborn soon,

Best moment for the mom, great boon,


Scar sure to pinch for a few days,

Joy of motherhood, the ultimate they say,


C Section is an alternate route of birth,

With modern medicine, it's a blessing on earth.

To save the newborns, it's worth.

# Anti-abortion law

Suppression of women again legally,
Save them, let them live peacefully,


Her body is her property
None should claim authority,


Her sex life is her liberty,
Will others keep silence, not their priority,


Will she keep her fetus, with none to support,
Without a stable life partner, where will she report?


Her body rules never to become law,
Who has the right to find any flaw,


Her right  for education, voting,
Right to hold top posts ,
She is entitled to decide about her body parts,


Such laws bind the teenagers to suffer,
Should they live with deep scars forever?
Abortion, euthanasia their individual choice,
With discretion, they can decide what they want, others never to voice,


Legislators have no authority on her,
Leave her alone, none to bother.

# Silent cry of an inpatient

He was a busy person,

Dealing with all, in his profession,

Summer, winter and all seasons,

Today admitted for a reason,

Treating doctors tell him in ration,

About his illness, add more confusion,


He is waiting for good solution,

For his disease, but gets no explanation,


His diagnosis not yet made,

He knows not his period of stay,

His day begins with nurses' entry,

Bed making ritual starts with fresh linen from laundry,


Next come the room cleaners,

Meticulously clean all the corners,

Canteen supplies him insipid food,

Carefully send him what is good,

He stomachs the same type of food,


His illness make his tastebuds die,

His appetite lost, making him cry,

He is sick of the same routine,

He gets claustrophobic in that room nineteen,

He longs to breathe fresh air,

He wants to see the morn sunshine,

He pines for his normal life,

All he does is lie and stare,

At all the walls, till he gets fine,


Silent cry of each patient,

None to heed, or heal his mind vacant.

# Doctor and non-doctor wife

Girl has no clue about doctors,

Marries a doctor, parents' dream fulfilled,

Dreams of the girl shattered,

(For) Doctor husband, only his surgical knife mattered,


Twenty four hours, he is married to the profession,

No time for romance, with cases in succession,


When he holds her hand, she never feels any passion,

While he counts her radial pulse's rate and rhythm with caution,


When he hugs her really tight,

He feels for the heart apex straight,


When she looks thru' his eyes,

He concentrates on her pupil size,


When they are into their intimate moments,

He tries to recollect his anatomy lessons,


An anesthetist looks for good iv access,

When he holds her hand, wonders if he would achieve success,


When he holds her neck his fingers feel for cricoid,

Can he palpate the cricothyroid membrane, she is annoyed,

Doctor husband fails to be romantic,

Doctor's wife never gets any kick.


More details cannot be put in words,

Stretch your imagination if you cared.

# Physicians then and now

Fifty years ago, family physician like a magician,

Treated overall, with compassion,

Those were the days of syrups, powders, simple medicines,


We waited with token, to get his darshan,

From dawn to dusk, he examined patients with no intermission,


Cough, cold, fever he treated with powdered medicine in papers,

His pharmacy though simple,

Had stocked relevant medicines, ample,


Those physicians were simple, charged pittance,

Their boards displayed no degrees,

They had wealth of experience,


Today's casualty doctor is only a traffic constable,

He constantly refers patients after making him stable,


Patient admitted in medical ward,

Poor guy sees a white coat, a great reward,


He is impressed by the magic touch of an intern,

Who takes history of four generations,

Patient waits for his turn,

To be touched by that healer gentleman,

Patient waits for days to know his diagnosis,

Confused by the small and the big doctors' daily discussions,


He waits to hear some words of comfort,

He has no clue about his treatment


Pulmonologist, cardiologist, urologist,

And many other specialists,

Visit serially, each criticizing the other's management,


Compassion today is surely missing,

Conversations totally confusing,

Care is an unknown feeling,

High tech machines detect all,

Clinical examination is absent overall.

# Anesthesia poems

# World Anesthesia Day

Days before 16th October 1846

Ways none to silence patients, doctors were in real fix


Barbaric methods cruel and horrible

Alcohol overdose hit on head inconceivable


Blessings to human race Bouquets to Morton

Sans whom trance sleep unknown


Ether, chloroform, trilene, halothane

Sweeter sure with 70s anesthesiologist

Curare, Flaxedil, pancuronium relaxants

Tough times travelled with all

Recovery slow, we saw overall

Complications many, GA was nightmare

No google, No system, carried bound books to refer


Atracurium, cis Atra, desflurane now

Awoke all soon to say "wow"

Available monitors around anesthesia now awesome


Smiling anesthesiologists, satisfied patients

Blessed we are with all cautions

Bagging stopped with workstations

Robot, Tele, smartphone, nano

Remote, sono, and auto too


None to replace our magical hands

Surgeons relax only if anesthetist stands


Future recoveries! Unsolved mysteries

Discoveries daily(older) drugs will be history

Rapid recoveries never shall we be jittery

# Ether

My good old friend dear ether
You were sure anesthetists' savior
Safety, security you always assured
Learnt anesthesia with you around

Pediatrics, geriatrics you were everywhere
Sure, saved us from difficult airways

Happy inductions we did always
Relaxed abdomens! Smiling surgeons!

No Mallampati no cormack
Got away easily with any tubes
No tensions, no anxieties very good days

Your sibling halothane born later
Stressed we were, safety shattered
Myocardium depressed; liver functions altered
Shivers and shakes really mattered
Though his inductions were faster

Your other sibling was trilene
Nay not happy with his blue shine

Lover boy, you died so early
Miss you dear very badly

Bottles seen on older machines

Nostalgia hits us with sweet memories

# Anesthesia

Related to all branches of medicine
Right from the basics to advanced pain medicine,


Physics is our basis,
Chemistry covered with logic
Organic and inorganic,
Biochemistry our pharma magic,


We anesthesiologists have all in our finger tips,
Memories sharp, reading never to stop or skip,


Anatomy applied in our practice,
All nerves of the brain, and spinal cord blocked by tactics,


Arteries carefully avoided,
Alternate imaging modality added,
Ultrasound whenever needed,
Complications well managed,


Physiology we learn of all systems,
Put into practice anesthetizing nervous system,
We learn and work with wisdom.


Microbiology makes its way,
Managing sepsis on some days,

Forensic medicine for dead ones,

Facing situations with critical patients,we witness some,


Medicine, we should be perfect,

For ,We are the physicians while the surgeon cuts,


Surgeon is our life partner,

We work in unison in operation theaters,

We have a love hate relationship forever,

But we cease to exist without each other,


Obstetricians are close to our heart,

They need us to attend to their patients really fast,

Keeping up timing on the dot,

We are each other's sweetheart,


We are connected with all specialties,

Omnipresent with super specialties,


We are the healers of pain overall,

Wherever and whenever we get a call,


We are the saviors of many lives,

Rendering basic and advanced support, they do thrive,


We are the proud anesthesiologists,

We put patients into trans sleep and recover with all methodologies.

# Human character traits, emotions

## Procrastination

A small defect in our genes?
Can be corrected by all means.

Habitual one of human race,
Happiness none, penalty he pays.

For dreamers of tomorrow,
Today is yesterday's tomorrow
They are engulfed in sorrow,
Heart is so hollow.

School homework of weekends,
When postponed to Mondays,
School students' sad mornings,

Start with sulk, with homework bulk,
Everything sucks, hell breaks loose,

Bills unpaid, bother us all,
Deadline extended, after all

Income tax calculations,
Man's worst botherations,
Mistakes many, bound to happen,
Mostly with procrastination

Annual check-up of health,

Delayed ones, cause sudden death


Doctors' appointment, attend with faith

For his words are Gospel of truth,

Topmost of "To do" list,

For they are never a myth


Falling in love, share with dear,

For delays further, someone can get near


Gratitudes to friends, hearty ones,

Go say it soon,

Lest we would be left with dejections


When we want to thank someone,

Wait for none, call it done


If our hearts are sorry for our deeds,

No hesitations, say it clear and loud


Procrastinations, path of downfall,

Time and tide wait for none, after all,

Our opportunity missed, to mend all

With destiny's call, death may befall,

With regrets at heart, peace departs

From us all.

# So what?

So what?

If I am always forgetful,

About my daily chores, still peaceful,


So what?

If I can't type the spellings right,

On my mobile, my specs out of sight,


So what?

If I don't understand technology,

I am good enough in my anaesthesiology.


So what?

If I am not meticulous,

On some deeds, never overzealous


Some say I have no mind for details,

Some others call me versatile,

With all views, I reconcile,


So what?


If i am not a great cook,

(For) I spent my life on medical books,

With no time to learn and look.

So what?


If I am not good at punctuations,

I concentrate on  my emotions,

I post Poems without confusion.


So what?

If I have no aesthetic sense,

I never end up doing any nonsense.


If I pass candid comments,

I may do at the wrong moments,

I respect their sentiments.


So what?


I was taken for a ride though,

Life's lessons, learnt as they go

Lost some dough, years ago.


So what?

I took the wrong train,

I landed at the wrong station,

I took them all as part of fun.


So what?

If i can't learn calculations of income tax,

I have an auditor, with suggestions of good packs.

And a husband who handles it, so I can relax


So what?

I have poor sense of direction,

I manage travel, with proper instructions.


So what?

If I can't load the dishwasher,

I wash them with hands, much faster.


I am proud of my veracity,

I am happy to possess tenacity,

I sure have some capacity,


I write moderately good  poems, in plenty,

I have that quality,

To take life as it comes, appreciating its beauty,


I laugh at my absurdities,

I move on with life, with some difficulties,


I sure have some creativity,

I also progress with positivity,

I consider them my precious properties.

# Sometimes

Sometimes

I like the day sunny,

When winter chillness is on me.

Sometimes

I love life's colours,

Which is full of surprises.

Sometimes,

I get depressed,

When my views are not heard.

Sometimes,

I feel very  blessed,

When i am being cared for.

Sometimes

I love those summer shower,

She cools the hot earth, we love her.

Sometimes,

I celebrate my success,

Followed by downpours, in excess.

Sometimes,

I enjoy the crowd around,

Sometimes I need my private space to surround.

Sometimes,

I treasure my pleasures,

When I have my leisure.

Sometimes,

I too get gloomy,

To cover the fume in me.

Sometimes,

I raise my voice too loud,

When I am not heard.

Sometimes,

I get too worked up,

When i am told to shut up.

Sometimes,

I dream of all happiness,

When I get them in small rations.

Sometimes,

I want to share all in my mind,

With a very dear friend.

Sometimes,

I encourage myself,

Showing my thumbs up.

Sometimes

I get disappointed,

When my work is not appreciated.

Sometimes,

I go overboard,

With trivial matters, if succeeded.

Sometimes,

I sulk with life's blues,

Until I see other hues.

Sometimes

I follow no norm,

But I see no harm.

Sometimes,

He answers my prayers,

At times, He doesn't, though rare.

Most of my days are awesome,

Some of them, I can't fathom.

# If only

If only I had wings to fly,

I would fly high, to make love with the sky.


If only I could blow like the wind,

I would push all the seasons behind.


If only the sun forgot to dawn,

What will the world be, with no morn,

If the moon and stars failed to appear,

On the blue sky, we would despair.


If the ocean stopped with no waves,

For a single day, it would be dismay.


If the palm and coconut trees were not so tall,

The tree climbers without jobs will be appalled.


If the wild animals were not caged,

Imagine the miseries the world would face.


If only water fails to fall in the waterfall,

How would the river flow with its riches to all.


If only I had the magical capacity

To heal all,

There will be no fatal call.

If I am endowed with super skills,
I will make everybody rich, hearts fill,

If only all those born on earth, to live forever,
For hundreds of years, with no fear,
Will there be space, for all on earth, not sure.

If only we were to remain young till death,
We will be making youthful blunders, to never become wise or clever.

If only our hormones secreted continuously,
Procreation of life will overflow earth, competitively,

If I can rectify my mistakes with a rewind button,
I would become a flawless person, to be certain.

Everything is created with a purpose,
We are all participants of the circus,
We leave the stage, after the show of success,
When the death bell rings we go,
No regrets.

None of His creations is immortal,
None can predict future and foretell,

"If only" is an unwanted wish,
Enough we have with total bliss.

# Happiness

We can find happiness all around,

With the daily happenings, without a sound,


To see the greenery of garden,

To enjoy nature's gift abundant,


Work gives us happiness,

When completed to perfection,

When we hear words of appreciation.


Though perfection is not synonymous with happiness,

Achievement is also not happiness,

For we can be happy,

With our imperfections.


Achievers are never contented,

Science researchers end up with resentment.

When their work goes unrecognised.


Happiness is not richness,

If so, the rich will never be sleepless,

Happiness is not success,

Success some see in excess.


Happiness is to enjoy simple things,

That we see in everything,

Happy when your pet dog jumps,

Happy to hear first cry of baby, when his heart thumps.


Literacy is not happiness,

Love alone is never happiness,

Are all learned ones happy?

Do all the lovers live in ecstasy?


Happiness is not a store gift,

Never comes in golden wrappers,

It is ubiquitous omnipotent,

In trivial matters,

It is the feel of the heart, never to part.


Happiness is humility,

Happiness is not achievement,

Happiness is plenty,

Happiness can be in poverty too,

Happiness is an indwelling one,

Happiness is novelty,

Sometimes gets in easy,

Seen in simplicity,

Some say it is sovereignty

PS: Last stanza ends with

H

A

P

P

I

N

E

S

S.

# Greed

Worst quality ingrained in some minds,
Wants more and more, in search of new find.


He who sows the seed(of greed),
He at the end reaps only weed.


When he wants to make a quick buck,
Ways he follows surely suck.


He has plenty, in black,
Hidden in many sacks.


Whites in his bank account,
With  security, safety, he can count.


Builds many buildings on earth,
(With) black money swindled, no dearth.


Earned from all wrong ways,
Ever too greedy, always.
Cash he possesses, nonetheless,
Countless sure, none from own success.


True citizens of the country,
Tax payers account their plenty.

Greedy ones' thirst,

Can never be quenched,

Even when fully drenched.


He is forever sad,

Heart gets scarred.


Farther, he goes to distant lands,

For he has mutiple hands,

Fixed accounts in Switzerland.


When death dawns on him,

With nothing he goes, only mourning hymn.


His wealth he takes none, no fame,

His name will be shamed,

His wrong deeds will be blamed,

His vices would surface, indeed,

His ills, selfish deals would be remembered,

His bad ones discussed, with no good deeds.

# Selfishness

He who is forever selfish,
He only cares for his own wish.


He is named" Narcissist",
Heeds only what suits him,
He does all in self-interest,
He is surely self-centered.


Forever thinks of his immediate family,
For they came through him only,
Forgets others, who travelled with him mostly.


He draws a small circle around,
Allows none, in his ground,
Unless you give him a pound.


Donkeys come last in english grammar,
I, My, me at the end, we were hammered.


Some states with excess water,
Share with none, though simple matter.


When natural calamities destroyed all,
We did nothing, watching TV from our hall.


With His grace we became doctors,

We protected ourselves, helped no sufferers,

When the pandemic struck our neighbors.


Some of them selfish souls,

Snatch others' chances cool.


In a crowded bus we sit tight,

Ignoring the challenged ones, pitiable sight.


We are smart to reserve lower birth of train compartments,

We refuse to share with elders, who cannot climb up the ladder, not important.

To mention a few of our selfish deeds,

Those shameful ones, with greed.


Steve Jobs named his products with an "i" prefix,

iphone, ipad, iview, iwatch, iclock

icloud to mention a few,

His "intention" was not a selfish move.

"internet" was their meaning, he was clever,

"I"conic ones, his products , forever.


Eyebrows, lashes too protect our eyes

Even they help others around

Never selfish, ever duty bound.


All of us are made with some selfish genes,

Arise we should for others' needs.

# Perfection

Seeking perfection is an aberration,

Some say it is an illusion.

Perfection is an expectation,

Putting heart and soul in full concentration.


Perfection is not excellence,

For excellence is only successful balance.


Perfection is an obsession,

Poor souls, who miss the pleasure of small imperfections,


No man is perfect to mention,

None without flaws, before their destinations.


A home is a home

Only with some confusions,

A perfect immaculate home,

Appears as a museum.


My handwriting was never perfect,

(But) managed to clear those tests,

My poems may not be perfect,

But my

Poetic lines are heartfelt.


Some imperfections are justified ones,

Lest life becomes monotonous,

Love the charm of being spontaneous,

Rigid masks of perfectionists,

Leave them with unnatural fit.

Perfection needs a vacation,

Please throw all prejudice and obstinacy

There is no justification,

For those who seek perfection,

Perfection becomes an infection,

A disease with no limitation,

It leaves a feeling of incompleteness

For some of them it is a burning passion.

Perfectionists fall sick very fast,

With illness of imperfection around their heart.

Evolution never possible with perfection though,

Don't make perfect an enemy of good enough so,

Life is beautiful, with less perfections,

Life is enjoyable, with no restrictions

# Ego

Many a ( wo) man born with ego,
Youth to old age they nurture as they grow,
(S)He remains the same, retains his (her)ego,
Wherever (s)he goes, (s)he never foregoes her ego,

The one with ego knows no love,
Keeps his (her) head high, never takes a bow,

(S)He knows not the meaning of humility,
His (Her)character is described as haughty,

Egoistic ones let out their anger,
Even if they know it lands them in danger,

Their minds have no place for others,
Hind brain full of self-bothers,

Bloated ego makes them complex,
Bursts like a balloon and it is shattered,

Egoistic one remains reclusive
Segregated from the rest of the universe,

With a simple apology they can mend relationships,
But ego deters them from making good friendships,

Ego makes them lonely,

Mixing with crowd, they miss what is lovely,


Ego is the fight between mind and heart,

Fail to see the difference till they depart,


Ego kills happiness,

Ego never to bring oneness,

Ego makes one keep a distance,

Even with loved ones, sheer nonsense,


Pride and ego are not virtues,

Put them away, free yourself from torture,

Ego is a constant enemy of the mind,

Shun it to become a different kind.

# Success

Success is a difficult journey on road,
With bumps and grooves, our journey slowed,

Success is everyone's goal,
To achieve it we put our heart and soul,

Success is not the materials of different sorts,
Success is not the possessions we sought,

Success is not the branded clothes we collected,
Success never lies in the properties we acquired.

Success is not our net bank balance,
Success we get facing challenges,

Success is not the degrees on paper,
Success never a gift with wrappers.

Success is not the wealth we possess,
Some make it from underground business.

Success of an infant with his first footsteps,
Success for a student, when he stands first on all tests.

Success for lovers, when their love is accepted,

By one and all, they are respected.


Success for farmers, field full of green produce,

Success for animals, with the prey they catch,

Success for those beggars, if they get two daily meals,

Success for a nurse, if her patients understand she cares.


Success for doctors, when patients are healed,

When critical ones get discharged, nice and clean.


Talking of success, may face many a failure in the process,

To face some failures, paves the pathway for success.


Success doesn't arrive overnight,

Hard work and vision make the future bright.


Success is a state of mind,

With deeds done, kind.

Success is a never-ending journey,

Successful: one can become at any age.


Success is certain, when we work with full zest,

Success is never a lucky draw; perseverance is a must.


Success is straightforwardness,

Never achieved by fraudulence

Key to success is proper education,

It is not just certification.

It should be accompanied by affection,

For fellow men, with abundant compassion.


Success at present, is for the world to become virus free,

Successful vaccinations of all to see,

We succeed only if this is achieved.

# Reunions

# After fifty-three years...

After fifty-three years,

We met in that holy Pondy town,

This was the place where we were fully grown,


That small town was our Mecca and Madina,

Had changed in all directions, we were in awe,


We were searching for that "Duplex Street",

With familiar shops and joints where we can eat,


We were lost, confused with the new town planning,

Beach was strange, but same old waves, jumping and greeting,


A batch which had sixty-five members,

More than forty met there, to remember,


Few we met, after fifty-three years,

With difficulty, we recognized our peers,

Although we were nearing seventy,

Enthusiasm at peak, we were still naughty,


Baldie boys, grey dyed girls,

Reminisced all, many sweet memories,


Amalgam of all types of friends,

Awesome few, at the peak of profession,

All in all, all faces glowed with contentment,

In whatever they chose to do, no resentment,


Few had retired after rendering full service,

Some still going on, never to tire,


Everybody was equal, none big or small,

Hearts rejoiced, nostalgia with pals,


Let's join hands for many future reunions,

Till we get His call from that holy Heaven.

## Reunion- part1

Reunions


Medical college reunions,

Met with all, memorable ones


Mails received from the organizers,

Meet up planned for the twenty fifth year reunion


Enthusiasm raced through, sky high,

Energies saved, awaiting the day


Friends flew from around the world,

Friends many, drove on the road,

Fancy cars brought, from far and wide,

Feeling of pride, nothing to hide


(We)Gathered for lunch, at a restaurant,

Girls and guys flamboyant


When each classmate drifted in,

We sure had great fun identifying everyone


Lanky lads, ladies of college days,

Loaded kilos, dorsal, ventral and sideways


Chubby ones of yester years,

Changed totally, with their aerobics sure

Boys of the student days,
Baldies mostly with very little hair

A guy totally transformed, attire shocked,
Roots into religion, he sure rocked

Studious, some girls of the class,
Stayed home, that was their choice,
Sleepy friends of the class
Happy, successful on the professional ladder

Handsome heartthrob of the class girls,
Had no charm, lost in life's ripples
Playful ones of the class,
Proved to be great, in the years that passed

Cool guy of the class,
Cardiologist now, taking care of the coronaries
Warming up the hearts

Best ones of the class,
Babysit their grand kids,
Profession takes a back seat

Few of us met though in various lands,
More the merrier, makes the union grand

Fortieth year we met again,

Friends gathered, with great strain

(With)Prosthetics in, cataracts out,

Pacemakers in, prostates out,

Hearing aids in, ears, power glasses stout

Sugar in, vigour out,

False teeth in, most teeth out

Silence observed for the departed ones

Sure to see some, till the platinum one

Grays dyed; Face wrinkles fixed (sort of)

Success stories, some shared,

Failure none, For all chosen paths' fun and fair

Spouses gathered, chattered all day,

On the achievements of their beloved, no way,

A girl and a boy who were poles apart, (of the class)

Destiny united them, never to part

Golden reunion, when will it happen?

Sadden us no more, spirits already dampened

Hope to meet all

At least by next fall

# Golden reunion at last part 2

Happening now, after three years,

Hearts filled with cheers,


Thought of meeting all in that memorable city,

All ladies plan to dress in uniformity,

Hoping to look pretty at seventy,


T- shirts ready for our city tour,

Teachers and taught to meet, emotions would pour,


Enthusiasm races up again in anticipation,

Everlasting friends, in for celebration,


Alma mater, so dear,

Friends to gather from far and near,

Awesome meet, to go down the memory lane,

With memories of life, when we were insane,


Platinum jubilee is far away,

Pray not to live upto that day,

Peaceful end should engulf us with no delay.

# Family reunions

Every year we had one, with fun,
Either in America, or India, sure done,


With daughters, grand kids, cousins, nephews, nieces,
We reminisced, good old memories,
Of our childhood, with extended families.


We tried tracing the family tree,
We knew not great grand father's name from memory,
We could trace a few members from
Every generation,
We got confused with some relatives.


Funny it was to learn that my mom was elder than her mama,
His wife(aunt) younger than amma,


Stories passed on to our younger generations,
Who lived theirs, in nuclear families,
Missed the happiness of joint families,


Recent generations with different skin tones,
Result of mixed marriages, white and bright they shone,
Reached out to each other as one.


Reunions in India, we sure had some,
Ran into each other, during weddings, functions to get warm.

Remained in groups, a swarm.

Glued with each other, instantaneously,
Got together, merrily, spontaneously.

Although we live miles apart,
We mingle with jingles, to chat and start,
From where we left last,

Family tree, gets strong with reunions,
From far and near, we travel, it's a great phenomenon.

Family members like links of a chain,
Fun and frolic, forever remain.
Family tree has a common root,
Branches though many, with occasional dispute,

Virus has segregated us all,
Visits curtailed of families, overall,
We hope to meet one and all,
Within few months, we shall,
See all, for we are social animals, after all.

# Gadgets

# Solar energy

Sun God's unique gift to mankind
Cheapest source of light and sound
Source of food, for plants, trees around
Science named it photosynthesis

Solar electricity, blessed by Sun God
Stored in solar heaters, solar batteries
Solar lights, glitter during nights
Sea water separates, salt free by solar
Saves cost too, separate chapter

Solar ventilation, through our wall
Sun God sure will be a source of all
Spread the word, to one and all

Series of solar lamps, planted in my garden
Solar lamps from dollar store, saved few dollars when sale was on
Source of happiness, as they start to light up
Spread, share life as they brighten.

# Online classes

My six-year-old grandson,

Learnt lessons about quarantine,

His mama prepared for classes online,

He was excited, the first time.


Online classes going on for years,

He was stuck with boredom, with no cheer,


Hours of watching computer screen,

He became dull, lost his sheen,

Every room into a zoom,

Doctors call it computer vision syndrome,


Parents opine it's a great blessing,

Portions covered, no time wasting,


Schools feel it's a good alternative,

Missing no lessons, their prime objective.


Distant learning was the way to go,

For the past many months or so,


Some small hurdles they do cross,

With mike fail, net slows, contact lost,


Students promoted to next class,

Not missing academics, sure all pass.


Schools reopened, kids happy with buddies,

Take all precautions, back into studies,


School going, their best routine,

School activities, umpteen,

Sports, playing and all activities,

Those rascals, lasses enjoy their connectivity.


All parents wait for kid vaccine,

Spare the little ones, and the teens,

Vanish you virus, stop being mean,

Make the world nice and clean.

# Smart phones

Smart phone has become a part of human body,
Some kids forget even mommy and daddy,

It has become an indispensable gadget,
Stuck in the jeans' back pocket,

It displaces the partner in bed,
It sticks to us, till we are dead,

Blinks, messages day and night,
From watsapp groups, phone never out of sight,

Old age makes us wake up early,
To find someone online, we get pally,

Lovers' heaven to posess one,
Emotions shared with emojis, noticed by none,

Bedroom, bathroom everywhere,
Bride and groom chat, privacy taken care,

Encyclopedia in a mini form,
Ever enclosed in our palm,

It is surely teenagers' lifeline,

It is also oldies' heart line,


When we enter the world of cyberspace,

We forget all around us in this space,


Families have no reunions,

Facetime replaces all, with this invention,


They are not as smart as we call,

They can never function alone, like a battery doll,


Our constant companion, anywhere,

Continents apart, to find a cousin and share,


Safety apps for working women,

Save them from trouble, safety assured, with numbers given,


Money transactions made simple,

Makes life safe, with options plenty,


This tiny gadget makes life easy,

Travels made safe, with crowds crazy,


Smart phones make men zombies,

Handle them with care, calmly,


They are great contraptions,

Wonderful science invention,

We must use them with discretion,

Never to become an addiction,

Vague sites cause virus infection,

I end with a word of caution.

# Facebook

A book that is held with no hand,

Friends countless, like particles of sand,


Wonderful medium of communication,

With friends, relatives from every nation,


Long lost ones we try and unite,

Reconnect with all, in a minute,


Blogs of unknown are interesting to read,

Besties we become, a separate creed.


Unknown people form a group,

To learn all, forming a loop.


World news in our hand,

Even before we wake up and stand,


With connection of internet anywhere,

We read all, sitting somewhere,


Sellers of essentials, tell us the price,

Saves us the trouble of visiting shops.


With the simple touch of a finger,

We listen to good music, of famous singers.

Lessons we learnt from Liverpool doctors,
Make us updated, learning all matters.

Misusers of Facebook, land in trouble,
Man's every discovery sees good and evil.

Manipulators make this medium dangerous,
Make the right choices, though tedious.

A constant companion at our old age,
When we have none, we speak a common language.

We had pen friends as students,
With whom we reconnect, memories abundant.

Face book sacred book for many,
To get likes from thousands, at the fag end of our journey,
Keeps us lively, even though we are "naanis" ( Hindi: grandma)

# Drones

Stingless male bees, mate with queen,
Simply gather no nectar, nor pollen,

They are the unmanned aerial vehicles,
They fly in the sky, making circles.

Ever so many applications,
Enter every zone, of population.

Aerial surveillance, Military vigilance,
Assist avalanche victims, with diligence.

Photography, cinematography assisting,
Agriculture, archealogy, by remote sensing.

Fire department to track wild fires,
Flying high, recording events of sky scrapers,

Biological sensors help farmers,
Bumble bee of drone, great roamers.

Rules abundant, to use these drones,
Restricted, prohibited every zone.

Types of drones, many of them,
Two to 250 kg, size of our palm some.

Pilotless automatic machines they are,

Power gas, electricity, sources from far.


Door delivery of groceries they do,

Operators from remote, with constant view.


Bird's eye view of buildings, beach,

Beneath sea, they rescue all with special reach.


Nano, micro, small, and heavy,

Single, multiple rotors, invent those tech savvy.


Indian government approved them in March '21,

Licenses, ownerships to be regulated soon.


Medical field benefits many to remember,

Medicines flown to locations remote, in slumber.


Organs fly to needy patients,

Over to them, only takes five full minutes.

Swiggy, blue dart contemplating delivery of food,

Some companies transfer all goods.


Drones enhance economy employment growth,

Danger zones, they dig in from south to north.


Eighteen to sixty-five are eligible owners,

Enable saving lives in natural disasters.


Wildlife conservation possible too,

With advanced technologies, lasers, range finders also.


Negatives of science, soon to spread,

Negotiations done, to halt illegal transactions.

Tasks completed from mundane to dangerous,

Twenty to 400 miles they move around.


Drones' sure boon to humanity,

Developments many with creativity,

Do their allotted duty.

Drones are the agile beauties.



P.S. 👆 1800 drones used at Tokyo national stadium to make it look like an image of earth.

# Aging technology for aging population

Technology has aged sky high,

Thanks to the inventor of wi- fi,


In the bygone days, big fat books that we carried,

It's now a blessing to be hands free,


Smart phone is a real smart gadget,

Rich, poor all possess suiting their budget,


All  sorts of information compressed in that rectangular piece,

Anything under the sun we get with ease,


Transactions, translations, television,

Together, students understand education,


Many more wonders, all done from one's home,

Mini gadget safeguards our home

Even while we roam,


Technology does keep aging,

Tech savvy people imbibe everything,


I am aging too, it's a sad truth,

I am good only with my steth,


My knowledge of technology is very basic,

My brain is wired with minimum logic,

Kids of present generation into all kinds of magic,

They understand even stuff that is robotic,


I am slow to figure out those apps,

I go really blank with google maps,

I wish I was born fifty years later,

To handle smart phone, and other gadgets,

Oh my God! Technology is sure a complicated matter.

# Google, YouTube

Why do I google?
When do I google?
What do I google?

For google is the answer for all,
For questions that are big and small.

Students' homework made so easy
Solving sums, life gets breezy.

Online classes of pandemic days,
Syllabus completed, no wasting years, they say.

No traffic jam for office goers,
No waste of time at those signals, though,
Morning rush scenes of every home,
Monday or Friday all days same.

Medical matters all on google,
Medicines, their details, minds boggle.

Post a query in a hurry,
Pat comes the answer from google dearie.

Dictionaries in all languages,
Doubts cleared, even at this age.

Those cookery shows on youtube channel,
Teach basics of cooking, sure novel.

Google our friend day and night,
Knowledge gained, we get bright.

You tube is a great app,
Webinars, seminars , workshops,
Watching them from miles of gap.

Teaches all, when we stall,
He is forever at our beck and call.

Takes us all to those state of art techniques,
To reach us from websites that are unique.

Liverpool doctor with his online demonstrations,
Learnt many matters, putting all into practice sitting in my nation.

America, Antartica , Botswana,
Africa, Afghanistan  or China,
Madurai, Chennai, Sholapur,
Mangalore, Mysore or Nagpur,
We may reside in any corner,
Google, youtube, with any foreigner.

We get connected to all kith and kin,

Worldwide they live, whom we have not seen.

Distill the filth, imbibe the good messages,
Defer dear kids, delete the adult matters.

Knowledge acquired, sure is a bounty,
Keep surfing google, joys aplenty.

# Clocks, watches

Constant companion, since childhood,

Ancient too, high on the wall,

Tightly hooked.


Regular duty to wind, wall clock,

Grandfather, uncles' daily task.


Pendulum clocks of yester years,

Ended never their work,

When wound by keys.


Soundless clocks, with uneven hands

Rounded shapes, rear encloses a single battery, works for years,


Digital clocks with red blinks,

Like a wide-eyed owl, occasional winks,

Double numbers bright to glow,

During midnight too, they do show.


Alarm clocks, were on the way,

Woke our students up, sharp to study.


Cutest of all, the cuckoo clock,

Cooing bird, comes out, it rocks,

Every hour coos and shuts,

Entertains all kids and adults.

Mobile alarm sure very handy,

Makes train travels easy,

Missing never our destinations in

A/cs(closed compartments)


Watches, we saw many branded ones,

Wow! None to match my first HMT one,

Worked for many years, with repairs none.


Styles, shapes changed over time,

Square, rectangle, wrist and pendants,

Some gold studded with diamonds,

Status symbol, of the moneyed ones.


Smart watch of current days,

Showing ecg, and pulse rates,

Safety features sure it has.


Amazing guy our dear clock,

Racing away with three strong hands.


Sharp at twelve o'clock both hands kiss

Part again, peacefully never to fuss,

Do their duties without rest,

Day and night with great zest

Clocks teach us great morals,

Duties first, then wait for laurels.

# Miscellaneous

# Oxygen

Oxygen, oxygen, everywhere,
Twenty one percent in the air
But nay, none to spare

Thank you, dear plant kingdom
For we breathe in, what you breathe out
Mankind saved, thank His wisdom

Our country poor in many aspects
Surviving sure with great prospects
Man-kind unkind, to you(oxygen) all along
Thanked you never, for so long
Never realized, your precious presence around
Took you for granted, inflicting in you many a wound

Cylinder, tanks, pipes scarcity
Gas, liquid all your forms we had plenty
Water, food, other scarcities
Waded through, with tenacity
Will sure manage, oxygen scarcity
With the help of the Almighty

Flights bring you from Singapore country
Although she banned human entry
As-Salam-Alaikum, Saudi bhaijans
Thank you for your tank donations

Thou need no visa, no passport

Nay, No corona tests at any airport

Royal welcome to colourless odourless gas

Cross all borders, make it fast


Never to hear, news of death

Never should people die of oxygen dearth

God, Bless us to witness a bright new dawn

Stop the pandemic, please you can

# Flight cancellation

With cancelled flights, we are disheartened

Connected families, across the whole world

Those grey, white winged birds

Heard us always, they really cared

Moments of takeoff, excitement mounted


Emirates, Qatar many to name

One or the other put us in her belly

With care, caution, flew swiftly

With friendly airlines, we flew around happily


A new star born in our family

In that distant maple land, sure she is bubbly

Pandemic punished us too badly

Cancelled flights, sitting tight sadly


(Our)Baby grew up to complete one

Frisbee she throws from maple land

Waiting for us, to catch with both hands

All her pranks, we witness on facetime,

Will He help us hold her, real time


Two more kids, await us

Dear little ones, pray hard,

For He answers kids' prayers

We continue to wait for the new dawn

Have mercy on us, Lord, Be quick to lift all bans

Help us to board our favourite flights

Patience we have, we will sure wait

# Will I become one?

Alzeimer's disease, all over the world,
Am I to suffer, Nay, I will be dead.


Nancy Reagan says "it's a long goodbye",
Never will I say, with my heart to cry.


Smart boss of a company,
Slowly forgets friends' names who accompany,
Rejects her favorites, not funny,
Dejected dear ones, so many.


Remembers nothing, gradually,
Recent members of society, get pally.


Skull encloses this box of mystery,
Sure, brain is wired with strange chemistry,
Still has dreams, soon to become past history.


When neurons die, millions of them,
With synapses disconnected, severed some,
Movements fumble, memories jumbled.


Where plaques, tangles, replace many a brain cell,
Way to go towards hell.


Stages of disease, they say ten,

Days, dates all forgotten.

Symptoms of early onset,

So many, eye is the start.


Vision impaired, earliest one,

(For) retinal screen is sure, window of brain.


Agitation, aggression, appetite loss,

Repetition, confusion, concentration lost.


Never tell her, her wrong doings,

For she suffers many a pang.


Birthdays of kids, grandkids forgotten,

Baffled she becomes, life gets rotten.


End stage disease, she loses inhibition,

End of life it is, we envision.

She ceases to live, only exists,

Let us not try to make her fully fit.


She needs no teaching on her daily chores,

Show her, hold her, reassure her more and more.


Till death comes to her,

Try with patience to help her.

I shall never become one, if God wills.

I will continue with great zeal.

# Adoption

Adoption is a noble deed, not fashion,
Adding a chosen one into their mansion.

God's decision to choose parents with dedication,
Gives away her son, when birth mother has no option,
Great parents who give them all, shower their affection.

Some do it as they have no choice,
Some good souls adopt to rejoice

As they got none, through married one,
Advice of specialists(infertility) they are done.

Lucky ones, those from orphanage,
Lord locates a suitable family,
Who never see them as extra baggage.

Their birth details are perfectly sealed,
Their bruises of heart quickly healed.

They do not have any birthdays,
They never bother, as they visualize
Secure pathways.

Painful sure, to part with her dear,(birth mom)

Proud she would be with his bright future.


Adoption Is a great notion,

For all of them, wandering as orphans.


Saving some from those predators,

Secure families they get through adoptions,

Solution found for God's children,

Successful they become, no more hindrance.

# Transgender duties

Transgender souls


They are the creation of God, His wonder,

They were churned in a blender,

They are the outcome of His blunders.


Genetic aberrations of mother nature,

Genderless they are of random mixtures


They are shunned by one and all,

Their families, none to call.


Thrown on the streets for being different,

Torn are their hearts, none to befriend.

Not their fault for what they are,

Nature's doing, God's own failure.


They have no place to go,

They have nil identity, oh! No!


They have no reservation,

They face only abomination,


Dragged into prostitution,

Destitutes, die with frustration.

They started some organisations,

They have their" Flag" demonstrations,

Designed by Monica Helus,

With blue, pink, white-stripe pieces

White in the centre denotes transition states.


Law at last named them third gender,

Leaving behind transgender.


Rose India's third gender lady,

Arose to become popular with beautiful body

Educated in foreign universities though,

Established on TV debut talk show,


They are born on the same earth,

They share the same air, till death,

They use the same water resources,

They get all from dear mother nature.


But we humans should become more humane,

(Never) belittle them, put them to shame.


Supreme court judgements of recent times,

Saving schemes, citizenship, Id, passports, they get,

They will sure be away from crimes,

If they are recognized by society, with all support.


Let's learn the truth of life, together,

With black and white, grey too is a special colour.

Every creation lives on earth,
"Eunuchs" should be free to breathe
"Challenged" ones have special places,
Changes should occur at a fast pace,
No discrimination should occur seeing their faces.

# American dreams

American dreams in

Many Indian students' dream,
Much before they graduate, they form teams.

Students from across the country,
Seem ambitious, to pursue their studies with assured entry.

End up with American universities, big and small,
Enough choices, they have overall.

GRE TOEFL exams they clear,
With flying colours, close to their American peers.

Onwards they fly from Indian subcontinent,
Over to master's degree, great achievement.

They learn to manage mostly all,
Accommodation, food, life before fall.

Those pupils pampered by parents,
Thrown into new world, no rants,
They manage their fees with part time jobs,
Those on campus ones, they are sure to grab,

Smart ones study with assistantship,

Stay in groups with good friendship,


Masters, PhD they graduate soon,

Make parents and country proud, sure a boon.


They decide to settle in that wonderland,

Their careers take them to many more lands,

What a country with plethora of opportunities,

With fifty states, welcome immigrants fortunately,


Visitors love that beautiful land,

Mountains, fountains, sea beaches, Disneyland,

Canyons, resorts, creeks, rivers, a rich land,

East coast, west coast, mainland, Inland,

Every stretch of land, feast to our eyes, when we land.


Stringent laws, straight forward people,

(To become) citizens, green cardholders, their prayer of Bible.


Hardwork, sincerity is all that is needed,

Happily appreciate immigrants' achievements, respected.


Social security for one and all,

Safe insurance, health care covered, no worry at all.


Senior citizens given great benefits,

Safety secured, with homes they fit.

Sundar pichai, Kamala Harris, such successful ones,

Sure made India proud, standing tall.

Statue of liberty with torch,
San Francisco golden gate bridge with an arch
Some landmarks our eyes catch.

Bay area bubbling with Indian population,
Bow to you, for adopting our new generation.

Bother not about many religious practices,
Brotheren they are, with any religion with no restrictions.
Built many hindu temples in every state,
Bravo! America our second home, no debate.

Beautiful, bountiful, borderless America
Black president, vice president, great saga.

# Retirement joys and blues

Retirement joys and blues


Retirement for doctors, different from the rest,

Really retire late, in mid-seventies,

Rare workaholics, go into nineties

Serve their societies, to their best,


Retirement from government service,

(we)Land next day into private practice,


My service retirement was ten years ago,

Much awaited one, though

For I was served summons,

With many a funny G.O.


Miss the joys of countless" good morning's"

Miss the mega feeling,

Of seeing the nurses waiting,

With case-sheets, a daily routine,

Of the patients who needed expert opinions,

Proud I was with the Steth adorns


Experiences gained from government hospitals,

Expertise achieved, only from patients.


Done with all the grueling protocols,

Done with monotonous meeting in halls,

Done with the responsibilities of department,

Days of agony,

Defending juniors many.


As our profession deals with life and death,

Allow no errors of drugs, even if dealers suck,

As we give the last breath.


Retiring as Senior Chief,

Reached the peak, great relief.


Some days after retirement, were doldrums,

Some days fully packed, awesome,


Post retirement goals were set,

Plans of reviving old talents, with my best,

Plenty of temple visits, I did though, Some more to do as vowed.


Made sure to attend all academic gatherings,

Made me knowledgeable,

Keeping up with the recent happenings.


Of course, I am into all TV dramas,

pen some poems without commas,

"A poem a day" is now my daily mantra,


Our service of thirty years,

Retirement was a mix of joys and blues,

Retirement came  with some perks too,

Railway concessions, taxation perks, Ooh!

Retirement for medical professionals,

Never end, not seasonal,

They are new beginnings,

They call it C.M.E.,

Continuing medical education,

Into the new innings.

Retirement sure has many a blue,,

Retiring joyous is also true.

Retirement is not punishment,

Retirement is not confinement.

It is only a state of mind,

Each one experiences  a different  kind.

# Old is gold

Old is gold

Said the wise men, really bold,
Shriveled skin, wrinkled face, very old,
Hunched back, sloppy walk,
Memory lost, still old is gold,

Old wine, and antiques
Valued higher, preserved by all techniques,
Old music, songs still are unique,

Monuments, temples, statues,
Museums storing all structures,
Made exhibits of various cultures,

Man's special creations,
Pride of any nation,

They are very old,
But valued many folds,

Getting old is growing mature,
Caring, cool, composed and endure,
Content, calm with no contempt,
Forgive, forget the wrongs with noble thoughts,

Magnanimous, away from worldly pleasures,

Chewing the cud at leisure,

Old is gold, gems and diamond,
Wisdom sure attained with time

Old is to cherish and celebrate,
For aging is a one way road,
Choice to return is not ours, dude.

# On doing nothing

All along my day, I try to do something

Over and over doing the same things,

Oh! No! Not worth mentioning

I am the only old soul doing nothing


Sitting in the same corner

Sleeping in the same manner

Gazing at the same scenes

Hazy view, unsure of what they mean


Inanimate ones, sure do something

Television on the wall, totally lively, overall

Tube lights in my hall, too bright after all


Clocks click, everywhere cuckoo coos unaware

Trees sway beautifully, across my windows

Ever dutifully casting shadows

Evening breeze, eternal bliss

Enters stealthily through the venetian blinds


All creatures are into something

All animals around, always moving

All birds, incessant chirpings

Awesome lovebirds, sure speak sweet nothings

Allow me to do at least a few things

Almighty God! I am the one doing nothing

Answer my prayer I am begging

# Past, present, future

Past, present, future


Let us live in the present, most recent,

Past is far behind, never look back and repent,


Future is far ahead, far away from the current,

Futile effort to foresee and lament,


Today is the truth, good or bad,

rough or smooth,

Tomorrow may be better or bitter,

To be alive today, is a blessing from up there


Forget the past, move on fast,

Future is a query, never should we worry,


Today seems relevant, live to the fullest,

Tomorrow is irrelevant, may not be the best,


Live in the present,

Love each second,


Enjoy the beauty around,

God's gift on this ground,


Feast your eyes with the beauty of nature,

Count your blessings before your departure,

Present becomes tomorrow's past,

Today's beauty may not last,

Past is full of memories good and bad,

Some we cherish, some make us sad.

# It's ok

It's ok

It's ok if I look old,
Shrunken skin, greying hair,
Still i am gold,

It's ok if I am forgetful,
I use my reminder app, which is truthful,
To check passwords, data correctly,
It is not so awful

It's ok if I can't hear,
I have two earphones, help me hear loud and clear,

It's ok I can't climb up mountains and hills,
I enjoy the beauty around, sitting at the foothill,

It's ok, if I am not a great cook,
Youtube guides me, I take a look,
It's ok we do not have flashy possessions
We are contented with the available options,

It's ok, my career is coming to a halt,
I am better than the ones who never did start,
It's ok, I never studied abroad,
Practiced my profession, ethically with blessings of God,

It's ok, I am not trained in ultrasound and echo,

My ancient techniques, hold good, here I go,

It's ok if my poems have fallen flat,

I don't give up, continue to pen with a cheerful heart,

It's ok, not to be ok,

Life is filled with swings and sways.

# Count your blessings

Count your blessings


Blessed with all body parts,

Born with no defects, thank God,

Blessed with a beautiful family, swells my heart,

All members get what they want,


Born in a simple family,

With siblings, lived happily,

Money was scarce awfully,

Minded nothing, grew up cheerfully,


Blessed sure, to get into medical profession,

Climbed up the career ladder in succession,

You made me savior of human lives,

I am lucky, always counting Your blessings,


You gave us good longevity,

Nothing to complain, got all in plenty,

Thanksgiving is not a ritual,

Thank you for Your blessings, big and small,


I have nothing more to plead for,

I shall remain grateful, till i fall,

"count your blessings" I shall,

Help me to be the same, till You call.

## Second Childhood

Second childhood
Every human goes thru' a second childhood,
At the fag end of life, when memories cloud,

When he shrinks, his brain contracts, he simply exists,
Vision dimmed with all lens,
Hearing impaired even with aids,

He unburdens all from his shoulders,
His childhood returning, body shrunk and shriveled,

He craves for goodies, drools over all eats,
He is shy to ask for his needs,
Relates only with small children,
Shuns all, speaks less, emotions hidden,

With marriage does he get into another childhood?
Wife in place of mom, caring for his needs?

Let every oldie enjoy this second childhood,
Let the family be with him, never rude,

He longs to get a child's heart,
Though not the face, a difficult part,
Let us look forward to this leg of life,
Let our transition of this phase be pleasant and nice.

# Grey

Black and white are the solid colors,

Black denoting downside of emotions,

White indicating immaculate, clear devotion,


Grey is a color in between

It indicates uncertainty, Indecisive state of mind,

Grey matter of brain, is a different kind,


Black and white indicate maturity and wisdom,

Grey areas define confusion of the system,


Grey is neutral, sensible, dignified,

Grey is natural, central and accepted,

Mind is full of gray areas,

Matters of unclear facts,


Grey is a great emotion,

Good or bad, it is confusion,

Grey is an accepted color fusion,

To be unsure is not a wrong decision,


Grey is born when black and white mix,

In the right proportion, ratio not fixed,


Grey may not be the primary hue,

But when added to main colors it perfectly glues,

Grey eyed people have unique personality,

Makes them attractive, emphasizing their individuality,


My grey matter dictates me to pen this poem,

On the ambiguous color of grey,

May not be awesome.

# Our vehicles

My earliest memory of possessing one,

Is that of TVS50, after our marriage done,
That was the year nineteen eighty,
Our proud possession, that green beauty,

Next came our blue Vespa,
Now sitting quiet like an aged grandpa,
It is as old as our first daughter,
It brings back memories of fun and laughter,

Maruti 800, the first four-wheeler we bought,
Many trips short and long, we did a lot,

Next came the white beauty Maruti zen,
Nearly a quarter century we had loads of fun,

Next decades we were into luxury cars,
Never equaled our first love, our TVS 50 brought,

Our seventies, we possess twin cars,
Sans daughters, we no longer travel wide and far,

This generation kids possess all, baby cycles to cars,
Boys of our generation buoyant with bicycles,

Our first love, first kiss, first vehicle

Our hearts get emotional.

Words of the wise men,

We remember now and then.

My association with Dr.Prema started from our early childhood. I had fondly observed
vour and devotion to a task on hand, even as a young girl. Her keen observation, her
etic demeanour, her love for languages, besides her professional success as a medical
oner are the dazzling jewels in her crown. These attributes are seen meandering through
ems.


Her poems are a finale to her enriched mind and reflections of a lifetime experience - her
ing mind ever galloping to express them in her creations in a lucid and endearing style


-    P.K.Geetha

Made in the USA
Columbia, SC
14 November 2024

46169252R00067